Discovering

Jesus

through Asian eyes

discussion guide

Discovering Jesus through Asian eyes *Discussion Guide*
www.discovering-jesus.com

© South Asian Forum of the Evangelical Alliance 2014

Published by The Good Book Company 2014
The Good Book Company
Tel (UK): 0333 123 0880
Tel (US): 866 244 2165
Email (UK): info@thegoodbook.co.uk
Email (US): info@thegoodbook.com

Websites:
UK: www.thegoodbook.co.uk
North America: www.thegoodbook.com
Australia: www.thegoodbook.com.au
New Zealand: www.thegoodbook.co.nz

Evangelical Alliance
The Evangelical Alliance
176 Copenhagen Street
London N1 0ST

Unless indicated, all Scripture references are taken from the HOLY BIBLE, NEW INTERNATIONAL VERSION. Copyright © 1979, 1984, 2011 by Biblica. Used by permission.

ISBN: 9781909919181

Design by André Parker/ninefootone creative

Printed in the Czech Republic

Also available:
Jesus through Asian eyes *booklet*

Our thanks to the following people and organisations who have made the production of this book possible: Clive Thorne, Robin Thomson, Dr Manisha Diedrich, Sivakumar Rajagopalan, Afsar Ahmed, Matthew Irvine and Wien Fung. All Nations Christian Centre, Assemblies of God, Baptist Union of Great Britain, Bethany Faith Ministries, British Pakistani Christian Association, Christian Vision for Men, Chinese Church in London, Christianity Explored, Emmanuel Church Wimbledon, Global Connections, Greenford Baptist Church, Gujurati Christian Fellowship UK, Haddon Hall, Hope UK, Interserve, The Leprosy Mission England & Wales, London Baptist Association, London City Mission, Lighthouse International Church, Diocese of London (Church of England), Mahabba, Naujavan, New Life Masih Ghar, New Life Suwarta Sangat, Share Jesus International, The Good Book Company, The Redeemed Christian Church of God, Scottish Asian Christian Fellowship, South Asian Concern, Stanmore Baptist Church, Word of Life, World Harvest, World Venture, UCCF. Images in this booklet are stock photos; the people pictured are used for illustrative purposes only.

Contents

What is Christianity?

Is Christianity a Western religion?

Question 1 in Jesus through Asian eyes.

1. Which aspects of Western society do you think are Christian? For example, how much of what happens at Christmas is actually Christian? What about Western attitudes towards marriage and family?

2. Do you think that people can follow Christ only in the West or can anyone follow Him wherever they live? Do you know any non-Western Christians?

(Note: This comes from the story of the first Christians, written by Luke.)

³⁴Then Peter began to speak: "I now realise how true it is that God does not show favouritism ³⁵but accepts from every nation the one who fears him and does what is right. ³⁶You know the message God sent to the people of Israel, announcing the good news of peace through Jesus Christ, who is Lord of all. ³⁷You know what has happened through-out the province of Judea, beginning in Galilee after the baptism that John preached—³⁸how God anointed Jesus of Nazareth with the Holy Spirit and power, and how he went around doing good and healing all who were under the power of the devil, because God was with him. ³⁹We are witnesses of everything he did in the country of the Jews and in Jerusalem. They killed him by hanging him on a cross, ⁴⁰but God raised him from the dead on the third day and caused him to be seen. ⁴¹He was not seen by all the people, but by witnesses whom God had already chosen— by us who ate and drank with him after he rose from the dead. ⁴²He commanded us to preach to the people and to testify that he is the one whom God appointed as judge of the living and the dead. ⁴³All the prophets testify about him that everyone who believes in him receives forgiveness of sins through his name."

Dictionary

Peter (v 34): *One of Jesus' twelve closest friends and followers.*

Fear (v 35): *To honour and respect someone more than anyone or anything else. Here it doesn't mean to be afraid so that you hide from the person, but afraid of displeasing them, so that you obey them.*

Lord (v 36): *King.*

Judea, Galilee (v 37): *Areas in the land of Israel.*

The baptism that John preached (v 37): *John the Baptist was Jesus' cousin. He was sent by God to prepare people for Jesus and His teaching. John told people to turn away from wrong, and he baptised those who responded to his message. People were dipped in water by John to show that they wanted to change their lives.*

The devil (v 38): *God's enemy. The devil tries to spoil and destroy everything that comes from God.*

Preach (v 42): *To announce and teach the good news about Jesus Christ.*

Testify (v 42, 43): *To speak out about something that you have witnessed.*

3. Wouldn't a message from God be for everyone?

a. What does this passage tell us about Jesus' life and message?

Read: Matthew 24 v 14

(Note: This comes from the story of Jesus' life and work written by Matthew, one of his disciples.)

[Jesus said:] "This gospel of the kingdom will be preached in the whole world as a testimony to all nations, and then the end will come."

Dictionary

Gospel of the kingdom: *The good news about Jesus Christ.*

Testimony: *Evidence about the truth.*

b. Whom does God accept? Does He have any favourites (v 34-35)?

d. What is Jesus prophesying about His message?

c. Who can be forgiven (v 43)?

Summary

God has no favourites but accepts and forgives everyone who puts their trust in Jesus as their Lord and Saviour. Jesus commanded His message to be preached to all mankind and prophesied that this must happen before the world ends. This means that Christianity is not just a Western religion; following Jesus is for everyone from every ethnic group.

Manoj's story

In 2007 I was living the high life. I was a successful businessman, buying and selling blocks of apartments throughout the country.

However, as I entered the New Year, my good fortunes took a downturn. As the credit crunch set in, my property business began to wobble. But this paled into insignificance as my two-year-old son was suddenly taken severely ill with breathing difficulties.

Though I was a born-and-bred Hindu, I had never really practised my faith. I always thought Christianity was something that was more to do with Europeans and Americans than with Asians like me. But at school I had learned a little about the Christian faith, and it had resonated with me.

But as my wife and I sat in the hospital with my son's life slipping away before us, I had a powerful sense that God truly exists, and that He alone could help in our hour of need. All the while a Christian couple we had only recently befriended were praying for us.

On the fourth day the consultant came and told us our son was gravely ill—she seemed to be preparing us for the worst. An hour later, to everyone's utter astonishment, my son suddenly sat bolt upright in bed. We had witnessed what could only be described as a miracle.

I agreed with my wife that we should visit our local church to say thank you to our friends for their prayers. But as I met for the first time with real Christians who loved me and cared for me, and listened to teaching about Jesus from the Bible, I began a journey which challenged my previous perceptions and beliefs about life. I felt called to re-evaluate my life, and new values and priorities began to take shape. I discovered that there was a God who loved all and died for all. Within just a few weeks I found myself walking to the front of the church to commit my life to Jesus Christ.

My business is no longer what it was. But what does that matter? When I found Jesus, I found a new purpose in life.

Why are so many Christians not like Jesus?

Question 2 in Jesus through Asian eyes.

4. Do you think it is possible that people can belong to a religion without actually following it? Why do you think this would happen?

5. What do you think it means to follow a religion? What in your opinion is a "living faith"?

¹Then Jesus said to the crowds and to his disciples: ²"The teachers of the law and the Pharisees sit in Moses' seat. ³So you must be careful to do everything they tell you. But do not do what they do, for they do not practise what they preach. ⁴They tie up heavy, cumbersome loads and put them on other people's shoulders, but they themselves are not willing to lift a finger to move them. ⁵Everything they do is done for people to see: they make their phylacteries wide and the tassels on their garments long; ⁶they love the place of honour at banquets and the most important seats in the synagogues; ⁷they love to be greeted with respect in the market-places and to be called 'Rabbi' by others." ...

²³"Woe to you, teachers of the law and Pharisees, you hypocrites! You give a tenth of your spices—mint, dill and cumin. But you have neglected the more important matters of the law—justice, mercy and faithfulness. You should have practised the latter, without neglecting the former. ²⁴You blind guides! You strain out a gnat but swallow a camel."

Dictionary

Disciples (v 1): *Followers.*

Pharisees (v 2): *Jewish religious leaders who were very strict about keeping the religious laws.*

Moses (v 2): *A famous leader of Israel from history. Moses received the law from God and brought it to the people of Israel.*

Cumbersome (v 4): *Difficult to carry.*

Phylacteries (v 5): *Small leather boxes which contained texts from the law and were worn by Jewish men to show their devotion to God's law.*

Tassels (v 5): *A decorative edge on a piece of cloth.*

Synagogue (v 6): *A religious building where Jews met to learn from their holy books.*

Rabbi (v 7): *A Hebrew word meaning "Teacher".*

Hypocrites (v 23): *People who tell others what to do, but don't do that themselves.*

The latter (v 23): *The second thing mentioned (here, "justice, mercy and faithfulness").*

The former (v 23): *The first thing mentioned (here, giving a tenth of their spices to God).*

Gnat (v 24): *A tiny flying insect.*

6. Can people be outwardly religious but not follow from the heart?

a. What was wrong with the Jewish spiritual leaders?

b. Do you think we can be like this in any way?

Read Matthew 13 v 3-9 and 18-23

³Then [Jesus] told them many things in parables, saying: "A farmer went out to sow his seed. ⁴As he was scattering the seed, some fell along the path, and the birds came and ate it up. ⁵Some fell on rocky places, where it did not have much soil. It sprang up quickly, because the soil was shallow. ⁶But when the sun came up, the plants were scorched, and they withered because they had no root. ⁷Other seed fell among thorns, which grew up and choked the plants. ⁸Still other seed fell on good soil, where it produced a crop – a hundred, sixty or thirty times what was sown. ⁹Whoever has ears, let them hear."

¹⁸"Listen then to what the parable of the sower means: ¹⁹when anyone hears the message about the kingdom and does not understand it, the evil one comes and snatches away what was sown in their heart. This is the seed sown along the path. ²⁰The seed falling on rocky ground refers to someone who hears the word and at once receives it with joy. ²¹But since they have no root, they last only a short time. When trouble or persecution comes because of the word, they quickly fall away. ²²The seed falling among the thorns refers to someone who

hears the word, but the worries of this life and the deceitfulness of wealth choke the word, making it unfruitful. ²³But the seed falling on good soil refers to someone who hears the word and understands it. This is the one who produces a crop, yielding a hundred, sixty or thirty times what was sown."

Dictionary

Parable (v 3): *A story from everyday life which illustrates a spiritual truth.*

The kingdom (v 19): *The kingdom of heaven or God; all the people throughout history who are saved from their sins by Jesus' death, who are reconciled with God, and who live under the rule of King Jesus.*

The evil one (v 19): *God's enemy, the devil.*

The word (v 20): *God's message to humans, the good news about Jesus.*

c. What does the seed represent in the story?

d. What stops the "seed" from growing?

e. How do these things happen in everyday life?

Summary

People can be born into a religion without actually following it or having a living faith. Others can be outwardly strictly religious but inwardly unloving and unkind. Fear of trouble, worries or the distractions of worldly wealth or success can stop us from following God.

"You have searched me, Lord and you know me."

The Bible, Psalm 139 v 1

How can we relate to God?

How can I relate to God when He seems so distant?

Question 3 in Jesus through Asian eyes.

1. Do you feel that God is distant from you or near to you? Why do you think this is so?

2. What do you think would be the result if we were able to come near to God?

¹Surely the arm of the Lord is not too short to save, nor his ear too dull to hear. ²But your iniquities have separated you from your God; your sins have hidden his face from you, so that he will not hear.

Dictionary

Arm, ear (v 1), face (v 2): *This is picture language. God the Father doesn't have a physical arm or face. The "arm" is a picture of His power. The "ear" tells us that God hears us when we speak to him. The "face" is a picture of the fact that we do not have a loving relationship with God.*

Iniquities (v 2): *Another word for "sins".*

a. What separates us from God?

b. What is the effect of this separation?

c. Is the problem ours or God's?

7 "Ask and it will be given to you; seek and you will find; knock and the door will be opened to you. 8For everyone who asks receives; the one who seeks finds; and to the one who knocks, the door will be opened. 9Which of you, if your son asks for bread, will give him a stone? 10Or if he asks for a fish, will give him a snake? 11If you, then, though you are evil, know how to give good gifts to your children, how much more will your Father in heaven give good gifts to those who ask him!"

d. Even though we have been separated from God because of our sin, what does Jesus invite us to do to come nearer to God?

e. How might we do this in practice?

f. What does God promise if we do this?

Summary:

Our sins and evil mean that we are separated from God. But God promises to respond when we seek him.

How can a good God allow evil and suffering?

Question 4 in Jesus through Asian eyes.

4. What do you think is the cause of most human suffering in the world today?

5. If God wanted to stop evil and suffering, what do you think He would have to do to stop it completely?

(Note: This comes from the first book of the Bible.)

⁵The Lᴏʀᴅ saw how great the wickedness of the human race had become on the earth, and that every inclination of the thoughts of the human heart was only evil all the time. ⁶The Lᴏʀᴅ regretted that he had made human beings on the earth, and his heart was deeply troubled.

Dictionary

Inclination (v 5): *Preference.*

a. What does this passage say about how God views evil?

(Note: This comes from the story of Jesus' life and work written by John, one of Jesus' disciples.)

²⁵Jesus said ... "I am the resurrection and the life. The one who believes in me will live, even though they die."...

³²When Mary reached the place where Jesus was and saw him, she fell at his feet and said, "Lord, if you had been here, my brother would not have died." ³³When Jesus saw her weeping, and the Jews who had come along with her also weeping, he was deeply moved in spirit and troubled. ³⁴"Where have you laid him?" he asked. "Come and see, Lord," they replied. ³⁵Jesus wept. ³⁶Then the Jews said, "See how he loved him!" ³⁷ But some of them said, "Could not he who opened the eyes of the blind man have kept this man from dying?" ³⁸Jesus, once more deeply moved, came to the tomb. It was a cave with a stone laid across the entrance. ³⁹"Take away the stone," he said. "But Lord," said Martha, the sister of the dead man, "by this time there is a bad odour, for he has been there four days." ⁴⁰Then Jesus said, "Did I not tell you that if you believe, you will see the glory of God?" ⁴¹So they took away the stone. Then Jesus looked up and said, "Father, I thank you that you have heard me. ⁴²I

knew that you always hear me, but I said this for the benefit of the people standing here, that they may believe that you sent me." ⁴³When he had said this, Jesus called in a loud voice, "Lazarus, come out!" ⁴⁴The dead man came out, his hands and feet wrapped with strips of linen, and a cloth round his face. Jesus said to them, "Take off the grave clothes and let him go."

Dictionary

Mary (v 32): *This isn't Jesus' mother but a friend of Jesus.*

Martha (v 39), Lazarus (v 43): *The sister and the brother of Mary.*

b. Why did Jesus not stop this man from dying and prevent all the suffering?

c. How did Jesus react when He saw the people weeping and mourning (verses 32-35)?

d. What did Jesus do in this situation (verses 41-44)?

(Note: This comes from the last book of the Bible, written by John after he saw a vision about the end of history.)

[1]Then I saw "a new heaven and a new earth," for the first heaven and the first earth had passed away, and there was no longer any sea. [2]I saw the Holy City, the new Jerusalem, coming down out of heaven from God, prepared as a bride beautifully dressed for her husband. [3]And I heard a loud voice from the throne saying, "Look! God's dwelling-place is now among the people, and he will dwell with them. They will be his people, and God himself will be with them and be their God. [4]He will wipe every tear from their eyes. There will be no more death or mourning or crying or pain, for the old order of things has passed away." [5]He who was seated on the throne said, "I am making everything new!" Then he said, "Write this down, for these words are trustworthy and true." [6]He said to me: "It is done. I am the Alpha and the Omega, the Beginning and the End. To the thirsty I will give water without cost from the spring of the water of life. [7]Those who are victorious will inherit all this, and I will be their God and they will be my children. [8]But the cowardly, the unbelieving, the vile, the murderers, the sexually immoral, those who practise magic arts, the idolaters and all liars—they will be consigned to the fiery lake of burning sulphur. This is the second death."

Dictionary

The Alpha and the Omega (v 6): *The first and last letters of the Greek alphabet, like A and Z.*

e. This passage says that God will create a new universe. What will it be like?

Summary:

Humanity is responsible for most of human suffering, and God feels immense sorrow and pain over it. He sorrows over the consequences of our wrongdoing and feels our pain with us. Jesus has the power to put things right and one day God will restore all goodness in a new and perfect universe.

Ruwini's story

I was taught that suffering is caused by bad karma from a previous birth. When I came across any difficulties in life such as illness, financial hardship and family issues, I then went after horoscopes, performed religious rituals and prayed to Buddha. I thought that this was part of life and something that I had to put up with.

I debated with Christian friends when they said that God created all mankind. I asked myself, "Can God really exist?" Then one day, I met a few friends for dinner. One of the ladies who joined the meal prayed for those who were present.

As we prayed together, I had a vision of Jesus. During the prayer, I felt a love that I had never felt before. He picked me up and carried me to a sea of love. I put my right hand on my heart, as I did not know where the love was pouring from, and I have not turned back from the presence of Jesus.

I now have a far greater sense of peace in my life, knowing that Jesus is walking the journey with me.

23

How do I know that God loves me? **3**

Does God love me?

Question 5 in Jesus through Asian eyes.

1. Think of someone that you believe loves you. What has made you believe this about them?

2. Do you feel that God loves you? What makes you think this?

(Note: This is a song written by David, a king of Israel and an ancestor of Jesus.)

¹The LORD is my shepherd, I lack nothing. ²He makes me lie down in green pastures, he leads me beside quiet waters, ³he refreshes my soul. He guides me along the right paths for his name's sake. ⁴Even though I walk through the darkest valley, I will fear no evil, for you are with me; your rod and your staff, they comfort me. ⁵You prepare a table before me in the presence of my enemies. You anoint my head with oil; my cup overflows. ⁶Surely your goodness and love will follow me all the days of my life, and I will dwell in the house of the LORD for ever.

3. How does God show His love for us?
   a. How is God's love for us expressed here?

Dictionary

Rod (v 4): *A heavy stick used by a shepherd as a weapon for protecting his sheep.*

Staff (v 4): *A shepherd's tool, used for catching, rescuing and guiding sheep.*

Anoint my head with oil (v 5): *In the Bible oil was used like this for a number of reasons: as medicine both for sick people and animals; to welcome a guest into your home; and as a sign that God had chosen someone to do a special job (eg: a priest or king).*

[Jesus said:] Greater love has no one than this: to lay down one's life for one's friends.

b. Why is it the greatest love for someone to die for their friends?

(Note: This comes from a letter written to the church in Rome by Paul, a Christian leader.)

⁶You see, at just the right time, when we were still powerless, Christ died for the ungodly. ⁷Very rarely will anyone die for a righteous person, though for a good person someone might possibly dare to die. ⁸But God demonstrates his own love for us in this: while we were still sinners, Christ died for us.

Dictionary

The ungodly (v 6): *People who do not listen to God or live as He commands.*

Righteous (v 7): *Someone who listens to God and seeks to live as He commands.*

c. In what way is God's love completely different from any human love?

d. Is there any greater or clearer way that God could have expressed His love for us?

Summary:

God shows His love for us in providing for us, refreshing us, leading and guiding us, and protecting us from evil all our lives. But the greatest way He has shown His love is by sending Jesus to save us from judgment by dying on the cross to pay the penalty for our sins.

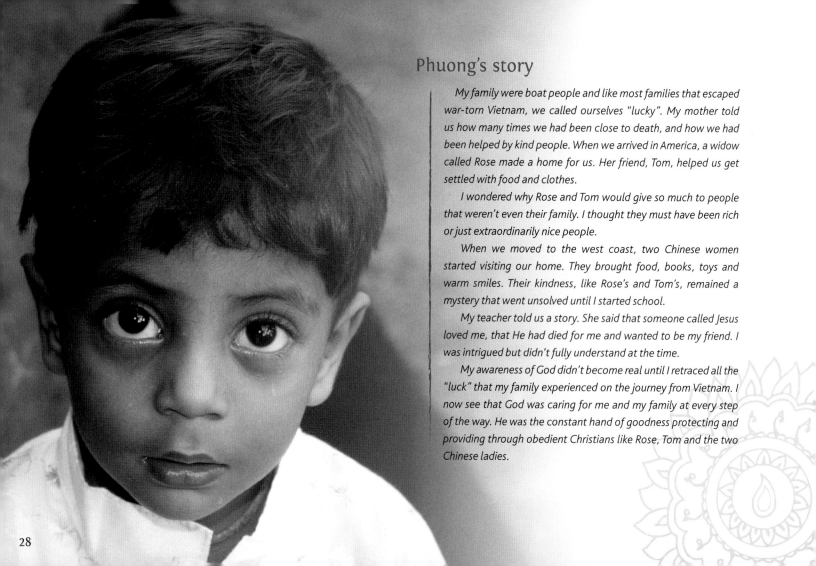

Phuong's story

My family were boat people and like most families that escaped war-torn Vietnam, we called ourselves "lucky". My mother told us how many times we had been close to death, and how we had been helped by kind people. When we arrived in America, a widow called Rose made a home for us. Her friend, Tom, helped us get settled with food and clothes.

I wondered why Rose and Tom would give so much to people that weren't even their family. I thought they must have been rich or just extraordinarily nice people.

When we moved to the west coast, two Chinese women started visiting our home. They brought food, books, toys and warm smiles. Their kindness, like Rose's and Tom's, remained a mystery that went unsolved until I started school.

My teacher told us a story. She said that someone called Jesus loved me, that He had died for me and wanted to be my friend. I was intrigued but didn't fully understand at the time.

My awareness of God didn't become real until I retraced all the "luck" that my family experienced on the journey from Vietnam. I now see that God was caring for me and my family at every step of the way. He was the constant hand of goodness protecting and providing through obedient Christians like Rose, Tom and the two Chinese ladies.

Why does God need a sacrifice to forgive sins?

Question 6 in Jesus through Asian eyes.

4. People are fined or sent to prison for breaking the law. What would be the consequences of breaking God's law?

5. If God did not require a penalty to be paid by the offender, would there be justice for the victims of crime or sin?

(Note: This passage comes from the Law of Moses, which was given by God to Israel in the Old Testament. It is part of the instructions for seeking forgiveness from God.)

27If any member of the community sins unintentionally and does what is forbidden in any of the Lord's commands, when they realise their guilt 28and the sin they have committed becomes known, they must bring as their offering for the sin they committed a female goat without defect. 29They are to lay their hand on the head of the sin offering and slaughter it at the place of the burnt offering. 30Then the priest is to take some of the blood with his finger and put it on the horns of the altar of burnt offering and pour out the rest of the blood at the base of the altar. 31They shall remove all the fat, just as the fat is removed from the fellowship offering, and the priest shall burn it on the altar as an aroma pleasing to the Lord. In this way the priest will make atonement for them, and they will be forgiven.

Dictionary

Sin/burnt/fellowship offering (v 29, 31): *Different types of offering to God. There were different reasons for these offerings and different instructions to follow when making them.*

Horns of the altar (v 30): *The square top of the altar (a sort of table where offerings were put) had corners that pointed upwards, called the horns.*

Make atonement (v 31): *Do something that brings peace with God and reconciliation with Him.*

6. What is the penalty that God has required to be paid for sin?
   a. How important would a female goat be for a family living in a community where everyone grew their own food?

   b. Why do you think that the animal had to die? What does this tell us about the consequences of sin?

(Note: Both this passage and the next one come from a letter in the New Testament to Christian churches. It explains how Christians should view the Law of Moses, now that Jesus Christ has come.)

The law requires that nearly everything be cleansed with blood, and without the shedding of blood, there is no forgiveness.

c. What does God require before He can forgive sins?

3But those sacrifices are an annual reminder of sins. 4It is impossible for the blood of bulls and goats to take away sins. 5Therefore, when Christ came into the world, he said:

"Sacrifice and offering you did not desire, but a body you prepared for me; 6with burnt offerings and sin offering you were not pleased. 7Then I said, 'Here I am—it is written about me in the scroll—I have come to do your will, my God.'"

8First he said, "Sacrifices and offerings, burnt offerings and sin offerings you did not desire, nor were you pleased with them"—though they were offered in accordance with the law. 9Then he said, "Here I am, I have come to do your will." He sets aside the first to establish the second. 10And by that will, we have been made holy through the sacrifice of the body of Jesus Christ once for all.

Dictionary

Those sacrifices (v 3): *The sacrifices made on the Day of Atonement (see Leviticus 16), which occurred once a year.*

Made holy (v 10): *Sins have been forgiven.*

d. Look at verse 3. What were the animal sacrifices able to do?

e. Look at verse 4. What was the problem with animal sacrifices? Why was God "not pleased" with them (v 6)?

Read 1 Peter 2 v 24

(Note: This comes from a letter written to Christians by Peter, one of Jesus' disciples.)

Jesus ... himself bore our sins in his body on the cross, so that we might die to sins and live for righteousness; 'by his wounds you have been healed.'

f. What is the real sacrifice that provides forgiveness for sins?

Summary:

A penalty has to be paid for sin; otherwise there would be no justice for the victims. God required animal sacrifices as symbolic reminders to people that their sins could only be forgiven through the cost of a life. Animal sacrifices were symbolic previews of the real sacrifice for sin, which was Jesus' death on the cross.

Jesus said: "I am the light of the world. Whoever follows me will never walk in darkness, but will have the light of life".

The Bible, John 8 v 12

Is there life after death?

What happens when we die?

Question 7 in Jesus through Asian eyes

1. What do you think Heaven is like? Do you think that there will be any evil or sin there at all?

2. Do you think that God will allow us into Heaven as we are or will we need to change? If so, how?

²²I did not see a temple in the city, because the Lord God Almighty and the Lamb are its temple. ²³The city does not need the sun or the moon to shine on it, for the glory of God gives it light, and the Lamb is its lamp. ²⁴The nations will walk by its light, and the kings of the earth will bring their splendour into it. ²⁵On no day will its gates ever be shut, for there will be no night there. ²⁶The glory and honour of the nations will be brought into it. ²⁷Nothing impure will ever enter it, nor will anyone who does what is shameful or deceitful, but only those whose names are written in the Lamb's book of life.

Dictionary

Temple (v 22): *The special building in Jerusalem where people in Israel worshipped God.*

The Lamb's book of life (v 27): *This will be explained in the questions below.*

3. Could anything impure or imperfect be allowed into Heaven?

a. What gives the light in Heaven? What does this mean?

b. Will anything impure ever enter it? What is excluded?

c. Who can enter Heaven?

The next day John saw Jesus coming towards him and said, "Look, the Lamb of God, who takes away the sin of the world!"

Summary:

Heaven is a perfect place where no evil can be allowed to enter, and so our sins have to be forgiven and we have to be made new in order to go there. This forgiveness and new life come through putting our trust in Jesus Christ as our Lord and Saviour.

d. Who is the Lamb (the one who was sacrificed to take away the sin of the world)?

How do we know all this is true? Only Jesus has come back from death to tell us this, and so we need to look carefully at the Bible's account of His resurrection.

e. What does it mean to be in the Lamb's book of life (Revelation 21 v 27)?

"Christ died for our sins ... he was buried ... he was raised on the third day ... he appeared to more than five hundred of the brothers and sisters at the same time, most of whom are still living."

The Bible, 1 Corinthians 15 v 3-6

Did Jesus really rise from the dead?

Question 8 in Jesus through Asian eyes.

4. If you were one of the disciples, what might you have felt when Jesus was arrested, tried and executed?

5. Do you think that anyone seriously expected Jesus to come back from the dead?

(Spoken by Peter, one of Jesus' twelve disciples)

22"Fellow Israelites, listen to this: Jesus of Nazareth was a man accredited by God to you by miracles, wonders and signs, which God did among you through him, as you yourselves know. 23This man was handed over to you by God's deliberate plan and foreknowledge; and you, with the help of wicked men, put him to death by nailing him to the cross. 24But God raised him from the dead, freeing him from the agony of death, because it was impossible for death to keep its hold on him. 25David said about him:

"'I saw the Lord always before me.
   Because he is at my right hand,
    I will not be shaken.
26Therefore my heart is glad and my tongue rejoices;
   my body also will rest in hope,
27because you will not abandon me to
      the realm of the dead,
    you will not let your holy one see decay.
28You have made known to me the paths of life;
    you will fill me with joy in your presence.'
29'Fellow Israelites, I can tell you confidently that the

patriarch David died and was buried, and his tomb is here to this day. 30But he was a prophet and knew that God had promised him on oath that he would place one of his descendants on his throne. 31Seeing what was to come, he spoke of the resurrection of the Messiah, that he was not abandoned to the realm of the dead, nor did his body see decay. 32God has raised this Jesus to life, and we are all witnesses of it. 33Exalted to the right hand of God, he has received from the Father the promised Holy Spirit and has poured out what you now see and hear. 34For David did not ascend to heaven, and yet he said,

"'The Lord said to my Lord:
   'Sit at my right hand
35until I make your enemies
     a footstool for your feet.'"

36'Therefore let all Israel be assured of this: God has made this Jesus, whom you crucified, both Lord and Messiah."

Dictionary

Nazareth (v 22): *The town where Jesus' family lived.*

The cross (v 23), crucified (v 36): *The famous Christian symbol of the cross comes from the way in which Jesus was killed; He was nailed to a wooden cross (crucified) and left to hang there until He died.*

David (v 25): *Israel's most famous king, and also a prophet; he lived about 1,000 years before Jesus, and wrote parts of the Bible such as many of the songs in the book of Psalms.*

Patriarch (v 29): *Male ancestor.*

Resurrection (v 31): *Becoming alive again after dying.*

Messiah (v 31): *Someone whom God promised to send, who would be a servant of God, a rescuer, and a king who would reign for ever. The Bible teaches that Jesus is the Messiah.*

The Father (v 33): *God, who is in heaven. He sent Jesus, the Messiah.*

The Holy Spirit (v 33): *God's Spirit, who has been given to those who follow Jesus Christ. He helps them to live in a way that pleases God and to teach people the message about Jesus Christ.*

The Lord said to my Lord (v 34): *God (the Lord) is speaking to someone who is king over King David (my Lord).*

6. What did the disciples say about Jesus' resurrection?
   a. What are the main points that Peter wants to communicate?

b. Peter quotes, in verses 25-28, a psalm written by King David about 1,000 years before Jesus. How does he show that this predicts Jesus' resurrection?

c. Peter quotes another psalm of David in verses 34-35. How does David's psalm, as explained by Peter, show that Jesus is Lord over creation?

Corinthians 15 v 3-20

(Note: This comes from a letter written by Paul to the church in Corinth. It is Paul's summary of several of Jesus' resurrection appearances, written around AD54, just 20 years after the events. It describes the message that the apostles had been preaching for all those years.)

[3]For what I received I passed on to you as of first importance: that Christ died for our sins according to the Scriptures, [4]that he was buried, that he was raised on the third day according to the Scriptures, [5]and that he appeared to Cephas, and then to the Twelve. [6]After that, he appeared to more than five hundred of the brothers and sisters at the same time, most of whom are still living, though some have fallen asleep. [7]Then he appeared to James, then to all the apostles, [8]and last of all he appeared to me also, as to one abnormally born.

[9]For I am the least of the apostles and do not even deserve to be called an apostle, because I persecuted the church of God. [10]But by the grace of God I am what I am, and his grace to me was not without effect. No, I worked harder than all of them – yet not I, but the grace of God that was with me. [11]Whether, then, it is I or they, this is what we preach, and this is what you believed.

¹²But if it is preached that Christ has been raised from the dead, how can some of you say that there is no resurrection of the dead? ¹³If there is no resurrection of the dead, then not even Christ has been raised. ¹⁴And if Christ has not been raised, our preaching is useless and so is your faith. ¹⁵More than that, we are then found to be false witnesses about God, for we have testified about God that he raised Christ from the dead. But he did not raise him if in fact the dead are not raised. ¹⁶For if the dead are not raised, then Christ has not been raised either. ¹⁷And if Christ has not been raised, your faith is futile; you are still in your sins. ¹⁸Then those also who have fallen asleep in Christ are lost. ¹⁹If only for this life we have hope in Christ, we are of all people most to be pitied.

²⁰But Christ has indeed been raised from the dead, the firstfruits of those who have fallen asleep.

Dictionary

Scriptures (v 3): *Here it means the Old Testament, the part of the Bible written before Jesus was born.*

Cephas (v 5): *"Peter" in the Aramaic language.*

The Twelve (v 5): *Twelve people Jesus chose who were the closest to Him.*

Brothers and sisters (v 6): *Followers of Jesus Christ.*

James (v 7): *Probably Jesus' brother, who became an important leader in the first church in Jerusalem.*

Apostles (v 7): *Those specially chosen by God to teach the message about Jesus Christ to the first Christians.*

Grace (v 10): *Undeserved kindness.*

Faith (v 14): *Trust in Jesus Christ to rescue us from the penalty of sin, so we can live with God in Heaven.*

Fallen asleep in Christ (v 18): *Because Christians who die go immediately to be with Jesus, the New Testament usually talks about Christians falling asleep, not dying.*

Firstfruits (v 20): *Just as the first fruit picked in summer shows that more fruit will follow, Jesus' resurrection shows that all Christians will one day be raised from the dead.*

d. Why do you think Paul describes Jesus' resurrection appearances as being at the heart of the message about Jesus?

f. Does the Christian message still work if the resurrection never happened?

e. Paul says that most of those people to whom Jesus appeared after His resurrection were still alive. What could his first readers do?

Summary:

The disciples were not expecting Jesus to rise from the dead, but afterwards they believed it had really happened. Their consistent message was that they had met with Him alive after His death. Jesus' resurrection formed the heart of the message about Jesus because it confirmed Jesus' claims to be the Messiah, the Saviour King promised by God in the Old Testament. Jesus' resurrection also showed that His sacrifice on the cross had paid the penalty for sin and had overcome death. Jesus is alive today and present with His followers to guide and protect them, and answer their prayers. He can open the way to God for all people.

"No one has ever seen God, but the one and only Son, who is Himself God and is in closest relationship with the Father, has made Him known."   The Bible, John 1 v 18

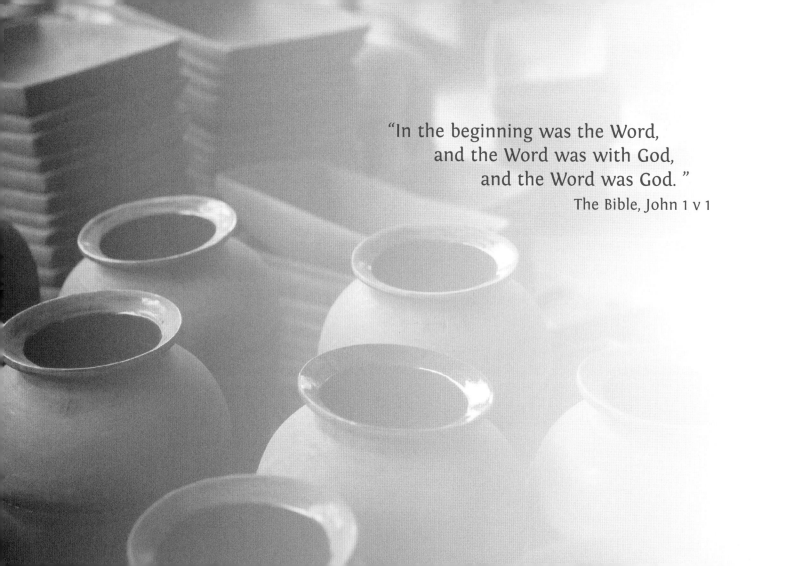

"In the beginning was the Word,
and the Word was with God,
and the Word was God. "

The Bible, John 1 v 1

Who is Jesus?

What do Christians mean by calling Jesus the "Son of God"?

Question 9 in Jesus through Asian eyes.

1. Jesus is the only person ever to be born without a biological human father. Why do you think God did this?

2. Have you ever used an expression: "Son of ..."? What did you mean by it?

(Note: This comes from the story of Jesus' life and work written by Luke.)

[26]In the sixth month of Elizabeth's pregnancy, God sent the angel Gabriel to Nazareth, a town in Galilee, [27]to a virgin pledged to be married to a man named Joseph, a descendant of David. The virgin's name was Mary. [28]The angel went to her and said, "Greetings, you who are highly favoured! The Lord is with you."

[29]Mary was greatly troubled at his words and wondered what kind of greeting this might be. [30]But the angel said to her, "Do not be afraid, Mary, you have found favour with God. [31]You will conceive and give birth to a son, and you are to call him Jesus. [32]He will be great and will be called the Son of the Most High. The Lord God will give him the throne of his father David, [33]and he will reign over Jacob's descendants for ever; his kingdom will never end."

[34]"How will this be," Mary asked the angel, "since I am a virgin?"

[35]The angel answered, "The Holy Spirit will come on you, and the power of the Most High will overshadow you. So the holy one to be born will be called the Son of God. [36]Even Elizabeth your relative is going to have a child in her old age, and she who was said to be unable to conceive is in her sixth month. [37]For no word from God will ever fail."

[38] "I am the Lord's servant," Mary answered. "May your word to me be fulfilled." Then the angel left her.

Dictionary

David (v 27): *King David, the human ancestor of Jesus, who was Israel's first true king.*

Jacob's descendants (v 33): *The people of Israel.*

3. What does the Bible teach about the meaning of the title "Son of God"?
   a. Why is Jesus to be called the "Son of God"?

b. It isn't naturally possible for a baby to be born without a biological human father. So what sign did God give Mary to show that His promise would come true?

Read John 10 v 30-38

[Jesus said:]

³⁰"I and the Father are one." ³¹Again his Jewish opponents picked up stones to stone him, ³²but Jesus said to them, "I have shown you many good works from the Father. For which of these do you stone me?" ³³"We are not stoning you for any good work," they replied, "but for blasphemy, because you, a mere man, claim to be God." ³⁴Jesus answered them, "Is it not written in your Law,

'I have said you are "gods"'? ³⁵If he called them "gods", to whom the word of God came—and Scripture cannot be set aside—³⁶what about the one whom the Father set apart as his very own and sent into the world? Why then do you accuse me of blasphemy because I said, 'I am God's Son'? ³⁷Do not believe me unless I do the works of my Father. ³⁸But if I do them, even though you do not believe me, believe the works, that you may know and understand that the Father is in me, and I in the Father."

Dictionary

Stoning (v 31-33): *In Israel at that time, the penalty for very bad crimes, including blasphemy, was to kill the person by throwing stones at them until they were dead.*

Blasphemy (v 33): *The crime of dishonouring God.*

c. Why did the Jews become angry enough to prepare to stone Jesus?

d. What is Jesus saying about His relationship with the Father by calling Himself God's Son? (See verses 30, 36 and 38.)

Summary:

Jesus is called the "Son of God" because He was born through the power of God and had no biological human father. He shares God's nature and is equal with God. He was sent by God and is one with Him.

Is Jesus really God?

Question 10 in Jesus through Asian eyes.

4. Do you think that there is any limit to what God can do? What could stop God taking human form if He wanted to?

5. If God did take human form, what do you think that man would be like?

Read John 14 v 8-11

[8]Philip said, "Lord, show us the Father and that will be enough for us."

[9]Jesus answered: "Don't you know me, Philip, even after I have been among you such a long time? Anyone who has seen me has seen the Father. How can you say, 'Show us the Father'? [10]Don't you believe that I am in the Father, and that the Father is in me? The words I say to you I do not speak on my own authority. Rather, it is the Father, living in me, who is doing his work. [11]Believe me when I say that I am in the Father and the Father is in me; or at least believe on the evidence of the works themselves."

Dictionary

Works (v 11): *Here, miracles.*

6. How does Jesus identify Himself?

a. What does Jesus' reply say about His relationship with God the Father?

b. Why does He say we should believe Him?

Read John 20 v 24-29

²⁴Now Thomas (also known as Didymus), one of the Twelve, was not with the disciples when Jesus came. ²⁵So the other disciples told him, "We have seen the Lord!" But he said to them, "Unless I see the nail marks in his hands and put my finger where the nails were, and put my hand into his side, I will not believe." ²⁶A week later his disciples were in the house again, and Thomas was with them. Though the doors were locked, Jesus came and stood among them and said, "Peace be with you!" ²⁷Then he said to Thomas, "Put your finger here; see my hands. Reach out your hand and put it into my side. Stop doubting and believe." ²⁸Thomas said to him, "My Lord and my God!" ²⁹Then Jesus told him, "Because you have seen me, you have believed; blessed are those who have not seen and yet have believed."

c. How does Jesus react when Thomas addresses Him as God?

Compare the following two Bible passages:

(1) Revelation 19 v 9-10

(Note: This is from the last book in the Bible, in which John has a vision of what heaven is like, and meets several angels.)

[9]Then the angel said to me, "Write this: Blessed are those who are invited to the wedding supper of the Lamb!" And he added, "These are the true words of God." [10]At this I fell at his feet to worship him. But he said to me, "Don't do that! I am a fellow servant with you and with your brothers and sisters who hold to the testimony of Jesus. Worship God! For it is the Spirit of prophecy who bears testimony to Jesus."

(2) Acts 14 v 11-15

(Note: Paul has just healed a lame man in the name of Jesus.)

[11]When the crowd saw what Paul had done, they shouted in the Lycaonian language, "The gods have come down to us in human form!" [12]Barnabas they called Zeus, and Paul they called Hermes because he was the chief speaker. [13]The priest of Zeus, whose temple was just outside the city, brought bulls and wreaths to the city gates because he and the crowd wanted to offer sacrifices to them. [14]But when the apostles Barnabas and Paul heard of this, they tore their clothes and rushed out into the crowd, shouting: [15] "Friends, why are you doing this? We too are only human, like you. We are bringing you good news, telling you to turn from these worthless things to the living God, who made the heavens and the earth and the sea and everything in them."

Dictionary

Paul (v 11): *An enemy of Christianity who was changed by God and became an apostle.*

Barnabas (v 12): *Paul's colleague.*

Zeus, Hermes (v 12): *Greek gods; Paul and Barnabas were in Greece at this time.*

Tore their clothes: *A sign that they thought what the people said was insulting to God.*

d. How is the reaction of the angel/men different from Jesus' reaction when someone tries to worship them?

e. What does this show us about Jesus?

Summary:

God is all-powerful and so nothing can stop Him taking human form if He wants to. We would expect such a man to live a perfect life and to have power over all nature. Jesus did these things and also clearly claimed to be God, by forgiving sins and accepting honour as God.

Song's story

I have always tried to be a good person. My parents brought me up to show charity and be nice to those around me. There is a Chinese saying that goes, "Do good and reap good". I was being a good person, and I was happy, but still, I could not help feeling a sense of emptiness when I asked myself, "What do I do all this for?"

I discovered that "doing good" does not always "reap good". There were times when it all went wrong; there were people that I cared for who repeatedly disappointed me.

Being a good person does not make you perfect or give you purpose in life.

I discovered that Christianity is not about being good, because we can never be good enough. It is about trusting Jesus, who gives us His perfection and paid for our sins on the cross.

As a follower of Jesus, I was able to clarify my reason for doing good. It is for the glory of God, instead of my own feel-good factor. I learned to be more caring with God's love, for He called us to love all our neighbours, and not just the ones we like. There is no use in being a good person without the love of God. And, in God, I know I will always reap good by following His will, for my treasure is in heaven.

Is Jesus the only way to reach God?  6

Isn't being a good person the most important thing?

Question 11 in Jesus through Asian eyes.

1. No one teaches their children to be selfish, greedy or naughty, so where do these urges come from?

   If such evil is in our human nature, how can we expect to change into those who do good?

2. Have you ever met a person who could correctly claim never to do, think or feel anything wrong?

   In the depths of your heart, do you think that you are good enough for God?

[Jesus said:] [38]"You have heard that it was said, 'Eye for eye, and tooth for tooth.' [39]But I tell you, do not resist an evil person. If anyone slaps you on the right cheek, turn to them the other cheek also. [40]And if anyone wants to sue you and take your shirt, hand over your coat as well. [41]If anyone forces you to go one mile, go with them two miles. [42]Give to the one who asks you, and do not turn away from the one who wants to borrow from you. [43]You have heard that it was said, 'Love your neighbour and hate your enemy.' [44]But I tell you, love your enemies and pray for those who persecute you, [45]that you may be children of your Father in heaven. He causes his sun to rise on the evil and the good, and sends rain on the righteous and the unrighteous. [46]If you love those who love you, what reward will you get? Are not even the tax collectors doing that? [47]And if you greet only your own people, what are you doing more than others? Do not even pagans do that? [48]Be perfect, therefore, as your heavenly Father is perfect."

Dictionary

Tax collectors (v 46): *A job that involved cheating people and being a traitor by working for the Romans, who ruled over Israel at that time.*

Pagans (v 47): *Here, people who believed in many gods.*

3. Who would be good enough for God?

a. How does Jesus command His followers to treat their enemies?

b. How many of us would do these things? How can we try to do them?

¹⁰As it is written: "There is no one righteous, not even one; ¹¹there is no one who understands; there is no one who seeks God. ¹²All have turned away, they have together become worthless; there is no one who does good, not even one." ¹³"Their throats are open graves; their tongues practise deceit." "The poison of vipers is on their lips." ¹⁴"Their mouths are full of cursing and bitterness." ¹⁵"Their feet are swift to shed blood; ¹⁶ruin and misery mark their ways, ¹⁷and the way of peace they do not know." ¹⁸"There is no fear of God before their eyes." ¹⁹Now we know that whatever the law says, it says to those who are under the law, so that every mouth may be silenced and the whole world held accountable to God. ²⁰Therefore no one will be declared righteous in God's sight by the works of the law; rather, through the law we become conscious of our sin.

²¹But now apart from the law the righteousness of God has been made known, to which the Law and the Prophets testify. ²²This righteousness is given through faith in Jesus Christ to all who believe. There is no difference between Jew and Gentile, ²³for all have sinned and fall short of the glory of God, ²⁴and all are justified freely by his grace through the redemption that came by Christ Jesus.

Dictionary

Righteous (v 10): *Here, it means good enough to be accepted by God.*

The law (v 19): *Here, God's law, given to Israel through Moses, which showed everyone how God wanted people to live.*

The Law and the Prophets (v 21): *The Old Testament part of the Bible.*

Gentile (v 22): *Anyone who is not a Jew.*

Justified (v 24): *Declared not guilty of sin.*

Redemption (v 24): *Paying a price to free someone from slavery.*

c. Does God consider that anyone is good enough according to His laws?

d. When we understand God's laws and standards, what does it make us realise?

f. How do we receive this?

e. What then is the way that God has made for us to be righteous and acceptable to Him?

Summary:

No one achieves God's standards in fulfilling His laws, so it is impossible for human beings to enter Heaven through their own efforts. God has provided the way for us to be forgiven through Jesus Christ dying to pay the penalty for our sins. We can receive this forgiveness and righteousness from God by putting our trust in Jesus.

Why do Christians say that Jesus is the only way to reach God?

Question 12 in Jesus through Asian eyes.

4. In order to answer this question, we need to remember what we have just learned about the problem we face as human beings. What is it that prevents us from coming to God?

a. Can we reach God by our own efforts?

5. The Bible says that Jesus took the punishment for our sins. Can you think of anyone else who has done anything like this?

³⁸Then Jesus said to them, "My soul is overwhelmed with sorrow to the point of death. Stay here and keep watch with me." ³⁹Going a little farther, he fell with his face to the ground and prayed, "My Father, if it is possible, may this cup be taken from me. Yet not as I will, but as you will."

Dictionary

Cup (v 39): *In the Old Testament God's anger and punishment of sin is sometimes described as a cup that is full of something horrible to drink.*

6. Why did Jesus say that He is the *only* way to God? Could there be an alternative?

a. What was Jesus asking here?

b. If there were another way to be right with God, would Jesus have had to die for our sins?

Read Acts 4 v 10-12

[Peter said:]

¹⁰"Then know this, you and all the people of Israel: it is by the name of Jesus Christ of Nazareth, whom you crucified but whom God raised from the dead, that this man stands before you healed. ¹¹Jesus is "the stone you builders rejected, which has become the cornerstone." ¹²Salvation is found in no one else, for there is no other name under heaven given to mankind by which we must be saved."

Dictionary

Cornerstone (v 11): *The most important stone in a building or structure. If the cornerstone is taken away, everything else will fall down.*

Salvation (v 12): *Being forgiven and rescued by God.*

c. Is there anyone else who can save mankind?

Summary:

Jesus lived a unique life from His birth to His resurrection. He is the only way that mankind can be forgiven and find the way to God because His death is the only sacrifice for our sins.

Jesus said: "I am the bread of life. Whoever comes to me will never go hungry, and whoever believes in me will never be thirsty".

The Bible, John 6 v 35

Is the Bible reliable?

Can we trust the Bible?

Question 13 in Jesus through Asian eyes.

1. Have you read any of the Bible before? What did you think of it? Has it influenced your life at all?

2. Did you know that there are two parts to the Bible? The Jewish part or Old Testament (which dates from about 1400-400BC) and the message of Jesus or New Testament (which dates from about AD48-96).

   Do you have any questions about the Bible?

Read 2 Peter 1 v 16, 19-21

Read Mark 13 v 31

[16]For we did not follow cleverly devised stories when we told you about the coming of our Lord Jesus Christ in power, but we were eye-witnesses of his majesty ...

[19]We also have the prophetic message as something completely reliable, and you will do well to pay attention to it, as to a light shining in a dark place, until the day dawns and the morning star rises in your hearts. [20]Above all, you must understand that no prophecy of Scripture came about by the prophet's own interpretation of things. [21]For prophecy never had its origin in the human will, but prophets, though human, spoke from God as they were carried along by the Holy Spirit.

Note: From the story of Jesus' life and work by Mark.

Jesus said:

"Heaven and earth will pass away, but my words will never pass away."

b. How certain is it that God's words cannot pass away or be changed?

3. What does the Bible say about itself?

   a. What does Peter claim for the Bible?

Let us look at one of the most famous prophecies in the Old Testament.

64

¹My God, my God, why have you forsaken me? Why are you so far from saving me, so far from my cries of anguish? ²My God, I cry out by day, but you do not answer, by night, but I find no rest ...

⁶But I am a worm and not a man, scorned by everyone, despised by the people. ⁷All who see me mock me; they hurl insults, shaking their heads. ⁸"He trusts in the Lord," they say, "let the Lord rescue him. Let him deliver him, since he delights in him." ...

¹²Many bulls surround me; strong bulls of Bashan encircle me. ¹³Roaring lions that tear their prey open their mouths wide against me. ¹⁴I am poured out like water, and all my bones are out of joint. My heart has turned to wax; it has melted within me. ¹⁵My mouth is dried up like a potsherd, and my tongue sticks to the roof of my mouth; you lay me in the dust of death. ¹⁶ Dogs surround me, a pack of villains encircles me; they pierce my hands and my feet. ¹⁷All my bones are on display; people stare and gloat over me. ¹⁸They divide my clothes among them and cast lots for my garment ...

²⁷All the ends of the earth will remember and turn to the Lord, and all the families of the nations will bow down before him, ²⁸for dominion belongs to the Lord and he rules over the nations. ²⁹All the rich of the earth will feast and worship; all who go down to the dust will kneel before him – those who cannot keep themselves alive. ³⁰Posterity will serve him; future generations will be told about the Lord. ³¹They will proclaim his righteousness, declaring to a people yet unborn: He has done it!

c. What prophecies about Jesus can you see in Psalm 22?

• Verse 1 (compare Matthew 27 v 46, describing Jesus' crucifixion)

> "About three in the afternoon Jesus cried out in a loud voice, *"Eli, Eli, lema sabachthani?'* (which means "My God, my God, why have you forsaken me?").

• Verses 7 and 8 (compare Matthew 27 v 43, the words of the Jewish religious leaders at the cross)

> "He trusts in God. Let God rescue him now if he wants him, for he said, 'I am the Son of God.'"

• Verses 14, 15 and 16 (compare with what happens to someone who is crucified)

• Verse 18 (compare Matthew 27 v 35)

> When they had crucified him, they divided up his clothes by casting lots.

• Verses 27-31

Summary:

The Bible claims to be God's word in both Old and New Testaments, and it contains impressive prophecies, which came true in detail centuries after they were written. It is a supernatural, God-given book, which needs to be taken seriously in all it says.

Hilal's story

I am a Pushtun from the north-west frontier of Pakistan and while working as a waiter, I met with a Christian man every week for about two years to discuss religion. I was hoping he would become a Muslim. Although I was 24 years old, sometimes my way of thinking was immature, and I would only hear what appealed to my own biased opinion where Christianity was concerned.

But as I read the Bible, Jesus came across as someone more than a prophet when it came to miracles. He told the lame to get up and walk, He made the blind see, He raised the dead to life, fed 5,000 people with a few loaves and fish, and spoke with authority about the forgiveness of sins.

Jesus was always said to be Al Masih, the Messiah, in the Qur'an, but it did not explain what that meant and neither did any of the commentaries I read.

Gradually, a change began to take place within my heart and I began to look more seriously into what the Bible says someone must do to get right with God. When I learned about the need for a personal relationship with God, I finally decided to trust my life to Jesus for His forgiveness, and I received new life through the power of God's Holy Spirit.

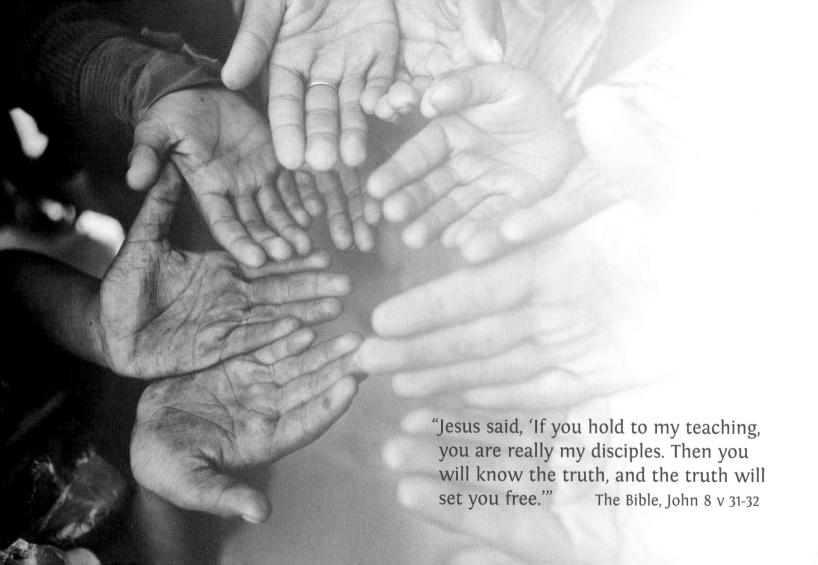

"Jesus said, 'If you hold to my teaching, you are really my disciples. Then you will know the truth, and the truth will set you free.'" The Bible, John 8 v 31-32

How should I respond if the Bible is true?

Question 14 in Jesus through Asian eyes.

4. What might stop someone from putting their faith in Jesus?

Read Ephesians 2 v 3

(This comes from a letter written by the apostle Paul to the church in Ephesus.)

All of us also lived among [the people of the world] at one time, gratifying the cravings of our flesh and following its desires and thoughts. Like the rest, we were by nature deserving of wrath.

Dictionary

Flesh (v 3): *human nature*
Wrath (v 3): *God's anger against wrongdoing*

5. What might make someone put their faith in Jesus?

6. How can we change?
   a. What is the root cause of our sinful behaviour?

b. If our very nature is sinful, how can we ever change?

c. How do we receive eternal life through Jesus?

Read John 3 v 16-18

¹⁶For God so loved the world that he gave his one and only Son, that whoever believes in him shall not perish but have eternal life. ¹⁷For God did not send his Son into the world to condemn the world, but to save the world through him. ¹⁸Whoever believes in him is not condemned, but whoever does not believe stands condemned already because they have not believed in the name of God's one and only Son.

d. Why are those who don't put faith in Jesus condemned?

Summary:

We should respond to God's love in sending Jesus to die for our sins by asking for His forgiveness, and entrusting ourselves to Jesus as our Saviour and as the Lord and Master of our lives.

Onkar's story

I was born in an ordinary Sikh family in Punjab, India. During my childhood I spent a lot of my time with sadhus (saints). I was taught that our chief spiritual need is salvation from our sins, and we can earn this by meditating, doing good and following a guru.

As I grew, I began to read the Sikh scriptures and do some good deeds and even got myself a guru. But deep inside I had a strong sense that all this was not enough to gain salvation.

When I moved to the UK, I established a successful business, but even though I had everything a man could wish for, I did not have peace in my heart.

Then one day, one of my staff gave me a Bible in Punjabi as a Christmas present. I took to reading it, and after three years of studying and asking questions, I learned that salvation is the free gift of God through faith in Jesus Christ to everyone, regardless of one's religious background or culture. Yet, I had been taught to do the opposite—do, do, do and hope for the best.

I was hugely torn between what I had learned from the Bible and my religious upbringing, and prayed to God for guidance. Some time later, I saw a vision: a light came from above and touched my forehead. God began to show me the way to Him.

Now it became clear to me that only Jesus can save me because God had sent Him to be the Saviour of the world.

Many years on I am a passionate believer in Jesus and have the peace I had always craved.

"Anyone who believes in Christ is a new creation. The old is gone! The new has come!"

The Bible, 2 Corinthians 5 v 17

What would need to change if I follow Jesus?

Isn't it better to follow the religion of my family?

Question 15 in Jesus through Asian eyes.

1. Why is a change of religion so controversial?

2. Following Jesus is often seen as a change of religious community but it is actually a change of heart. Is it good for a person to seek God sincerely and want to find God's way for themselves?

Jesus said:

"Anyone who loves their father or mother more than me is not worthy of me; anyone who loves their son or daughter more than me is not worthy of me."

3. Should seeking God take priority over family ties?

a. Why do you think Jesus says that we should love Him more than our parents or children?

46While Jesus was still talking to the crowd, his mother and brothers stood outside, wanting to speak to him. 47Someone told him, "Your mother and brothers are standing outside, wanting to speak to you." 48He replied to him, "Who is my mother, and who are my brothers?" 49Pointing to his disciples, he said, "Here are my mother and my brothers. 50For whoever does the will of my Father in heaven is my brother and sister and mother."

b. What do you think Jesus meant by calling His disciples His mother, brothers and sisters?

Summary:

Following Jesus is about a change of heart and belief, but it is often seen as a change of allegiance to the community, bringing dishonour to the extended family, even though this is certainly not intended. The almighty, perfect God is greater than our families and has loved us so much that He was willing to suffer and die to save us. Such love is greater than any human love and demands a greater response. Through Jesus, God calls us into a new family relationship with God and His people.

Jin's story

Whenever my step-grandmother asked my mother and me to join her at her church, our answer was, "No thanks—we have our own religion (Buddhism), and you have yours (Christianity). Let's just keep the lines clear and respect each other. Then everything will be good between us."

But as time went by, the relationship between my mother and stepfather became worse and worse—to the point where they were wanting to get divorced. I just couldn't bear to think that would be happening once again.

What little I knew of Christianity gave me an image of an all-powerful, all-loving God, and I was desperate to find out if He was really who everybody claimed Him to be.

So one night, I cried out, "God, if you're real, please save my family!"

Long story short, God listened to my prayer that night. He brought my mother and me to church, and gradually showed us through His people and His living word, the Bible, that He is indeed real, and He is unlike all the other religions that I have been exposed to. I discovered that Christianity is about a relationship with the Creator of the universe and the Saviour of our souls. The joy and freedom of this loving relationship is simply wonderful. But I would never have known this unless I had been willing to seek for myself the true desires of my heart.

Would I have to leave my family and culture to follow Jesus?

Question 16 in Jesus through Asian eyes.

4. What aspects of your family life and culture would be compatible with following Jesus?

5. Are there any cultural practices or family customs that you think would be incompatible with following Jesus?

Note: This is one of God's laws (the Ten Commandments) that he gave to his people in the Old Testament.

Honour your father and your mother, so that you may live long in the land the LORD your God is giving you.

6. How does God view family and culture?

  a. What do you think it means to honour your father and mother?

(Written by the apostle Paul.)

[19]Though I am free and belong to no one, I have made myself a slave to everyone, to win as many as possible. [20]To the Jews I became like a Jew, to win the Jews. To those under the law I became like one under the law (though I myself am not under the law), so as to win those under the law. [21]To those not having the law I became like one not having the law (though I am not free from God's law but am under Christ's law), so as to win those not having the law. [22]To the weak I became weak, to win the weak. I have become all things to all people so that by all possible means I might save some. [23]I do all this for the sake of the gospel, that I may share in its blessings.

Dictionary

Those under the law (v 20): *Jewish people who followed all the customs and practices of the law.*

Those not having the law (v 21): *Non-Jewish people.*

b. What is God's attitude to cultural customs?

c. What is your conclusion about what would have to change if you follow Jesus? Would you have to leave your family and culture?

Summary:

God wants us to continue to love and respect our families if we follow Jesus, and most cultural customs will be compatible with following Him, except for things that involve the worship of other gods or disobeying direct biblical commands.

Dear Lord God,

I turn away from living life my own way, from following other paths and from all the wrong things that I have done.

Forgive me through Jesus' death on the cross on my behalf.

I trust in Him to be my Saviour and Lord. Jesus, I give you all that I am and have, so that You may be the Lord and Master of my life for ever by the power of your Holy Spirit.

Amen

What next?

As you continue your journey you will find helpful resources, information and support from:

- **The website:** www.discovering-jesus.com

- **The book:** *Notes for the Journey*, which explores what it means in practice to follow Jesus as an Asian. Available from www.southasianconcern.org/resources/

- **The friends:** with whom you have been discussing this material

- **The Bible:** continue to read the Gospels, which tell the story of Jesus

- **Talking to God:** remember the promise of Jesus: *"Ask and it will be given to you; seek and you will find; knock and the door will be opened to you."* **Matthew 7 v 7**